SUMMARY

What does it take for a state to reform its police forces? In the post-Soviet space, the police remain one of the least-reformed government institutions, infamous for graft, collaboration with organized criminal groups, and human rights violations. The police still serve as a political instrument, even in more politically open countries. For countries that have embarked on police reform and, at the very least, sought to change the institution's name from "militsya" to "politsiya," suggesting a more Westernized understanding of the role of law-enforcement agencies, the change was made only in name, not in content. This monograph examines the forces driving police reform programs in former Soviet states and what leads to their success. Specifically, it examines a decade of reform efforts in Georgia and Kyrgyzstan from the perspective of political leaders, opposition forces, the homegrown nongovernmental organization community, and international actors.

The two cases were chosen to show two drastically different approaches to reform played out in countries facing arguably similar problems with state-crime links, dysfunctional governments, and corrupt police forces. Both Georgia and Kyrgyzstan have undergone dramatic political transformations since the early 2000s. Both saw regimes change and political power turnovers that led to more open governments and declining corruption rates. Both have received large U.S. aid packages for democratization projects. Amid this time of far-reaching political change, the issue of police reform became a cornerstone in the fight against corruption for both Tbilisi, Georgia, and Bishkek, Kyrgyzstan.

Georgia and Kyrgyzstan demonstrate that, for the change to take place, both top-down and bottom-up efforts are necessary. A political regime must feel accountable to the broader public to guide reform and destroy the Soviet legacy of a militarized police, while also introducing the public's voice into the discussion of how to proceed with the reform. Georgia and Kyrgyzstan each, however, lacked one of the two components. In Georgia, police reform programs redefined the role of the police in sustaining social order. However, these changes reflected the ideas of the educated elites, not the wider masses. The police-society dialogue is still lacking, and the possibility of future change is uncertain after Georgia elected a new parliament and appointed a new prime minister.

In Kyrgyzstan, the same old political elites who came to power as a result of two regime changes in 2005 and in 2010 have been trying to change the Interior Ministry by retraining personnel and amending the legal code. Political leaders were reluctant to introduce any major changes because many of them still had lucrative informal ties with Interior Ministry personnel. After many starts and stops and regime changes in Kyrgyzstan, the pace of reform quickened only after several local nongovernmental organizations (NGOs) inserted themselves in the process of designing and overseeing the reform in 2010-13. The future of the reform is still uncertain, but its concept has become a matter of broad public discussion with several activists and NGOs involved in the process.

This report concludes with recommending that U.S. military-to military assistance in Georgia and Kyrgyzstan must focus on training and sharing best practices regarding the separation of military and police functions and stripping the military of its political surveillance functions. A special panel/committee should be established to deal specifically with issues regarding the democratic reform of the security sector, and police reform must be part of that agenda. The U.S. European Command and U.S. Central Command must consistently promote institutional reform to eliminate such political barriers and to enable fruitful military-to-military cooperation. Potentially, Georgia and Kyrgyzstan could instruct other post-Soviet as well as Middle Eastern states about what leads to a consistent reform and what delays it.

REFORMING THE POLICE IN POST-SOVIET STATES:
GEORGIA AND KYRGYZSTAN

INTRODUCTION

Since 1991, all of the Soviet successor states have tried to restructure their inherited police forces, either to increase their capacity to protect the ruling regimes or to democratize law enforcement agencies as part of a broader political reform effort. In most cases, this included creating patrol police, cleaning up corruption, and changing the structure of the Interior Ministry. The states that underwent even the slowest police reform, like Azerbaijan and Russia, still sought to change the forces' name from "militsya" to "politsiya," suggesting a more Westernized, less martial, understanding of the role of law enforcement agencies. Georgia, Estonia, Latvia, and Lithuania are regarded as the most successful examples of police reform, while the failed efforts in Kyrgyzstan, Russia, and Kazakhstan, among others, have shown that merely training and equipping police officers will not lead to structural changes within the police force itself.[1]

This monograph examines the forces driving police reform programs in former Soviet states and what leads to their success. Specifically, it examines a decade of reform efforts in Georgia and Kyrgyzstan from the perspective of political leaders, opposition forces, the homegrown nongovernmental organization (NGO) community, and international actors. The two cases were chosen to show two drastically different approaches to reform played out in countries facing arguably similar problems with state-crime links, dysfunctional governments, and corrupt police forces.

Both Georgia and Kyrgyzstan have undergone dramatic political transformations since the early-2000s.[2] Both saw regimes change and political power turnovers that led to more open governments and declining corruption rates. Amid this time of far-reaching political change, the issue of police reform became a cornerstone in the fight against corruption for both Tbilisi and Bishkek.

Yet, while Georgia represents swift change with arguably limited external donor guidance but ample financing, Kyrgyzstan's futile efforts to reform the police included extensive donor involvement in the process. The success of the reform often measured with the changing levels of public trust in the police. In 2003, when reform began in Georgia, public trust in the police was roughly 10 percent; the latest survey, nearly a decade later, shows that 87 percent of people trust the police, while 98 percent said they never give bribes.[3] In Kyrgyzstan, public trust in the police has continued to decline over the years, despite international donors' prolonged support of reform efforts in the country.[4]

Georgia and Kyrgyzstan present an interesting comparison. While almost all post-Soviet countries have announced police reform programs, these two are the only states that have pursued the issue consistently for over a decade. In Georgia, the reform was implemented by the top political brass, while in Kyrgyzstan, Interior Ministry and civil society groups were entrusted to lead the reform. Both cases can boast of their respective strengths and weaknesses, with the Georgian model undoubtedly winning in terms of favorable results. In 2003, the Rose Revolution brought the new 36-year-old president, Mikheil Saakashvili, and a slew of even younger cadres into politics. In Kyrgyzstan, by contrast, two national regime changes merely recombined the same actors as they competed against each other or formed strategic alliances. Mikheil Saakashvili enjoyed strong popularity, and his efforts to combat organized crime and reform the police were widely supported by the public and the international community alike. In Kyrgyzstan, however, civil society activists trusted neither their political leaders' stated desire nor their ability to reform the police. None of the four presidents who have ruled Kyrgyzstan since the early-2000s was trusted by the NGO community to genuinely pursue reform, instead each was suspected of carrying out mere window dressing.

Finally, both have received large U.S. aid packages. The State Department's Bureau of International Narcotics and Law Enforcement (INL), for example, has spent over $65 million on law-enforcement and legal reform programs in Georgia[5] and $13.1 million in Kyrgyzstan.[6] Some U.S. Agency for International Development (USAID) programs have also focused on promoting democracy, reforming governance, improving the observance of the rule of law, and transforming the sector.

Potentially, Georgia and Kyrgyzstan could instruct other post-Soviet states about what leads to a consistent reform and what delays it. Both countries also demonstrate that for the change to take place, both top-down and bottom-up efforts are necessary. A political regime must feel accountable to the broader public to guide the reform and destroy the Soviet legacy of a militarized police, while also introducing the public's voice into the discussion of how to proceed with the reform. Georgia and Kyrgyzstan each, however, lacked one of the two components.

This report begins with an examination of what constitutes police reform in former Soviet states. It then discusses Georgia and Kyrgyzstan in more detail. Georgia's successful police reform demonstrates that political leadership's strong will to reduce corruption at the grassroots level can bring sizable results in a relatively short period of time. Georgia's case has its weaknesses that have stalled democratic development. Kyrgyzstan, on the other hand, demonstrates how external efforts are futile and cost-intensive because they seek to instill a culture of democratic police in authoritarian states. However, a protracted police reform program can engage the public's participation in changing the work of the Interior Ministry. The report concludes with the lessons learned from other former Soviet states and recommendations for the U.S. military-to-military engagement in Central Asia and South Caucasus.

WHAT CONSTITUTES POLICE REFORM

Police forces are a key link between state and society. At an individual level, the ordinary policeman walking his beat personifies the state's attitude toward its involvement in the daily life of its citizens.[7] Likewise, the society's treatment of the police reflects its view of the state. Police that use brute force against the citizenry or that embrace extralegal treatment of segments of society or specific individuals point to an authoritarian regime. By contrast, a society in which individuals attack the police, resort to bribery, and exhibit a lack of trust in law-enforcement agencies exposes the state's inability to maintain social order and provide security.

Essentially, the existence of a police reform program implies an effort to redefine the rationale for

4

police use of violence against civilians to maintain social order. It presumes that as states and societies democratize, the rates of violence exerted by the police against citizens, as well as among citizens themselves, will decrease.[8] The paths each country takes in transforming its law-enforcement sector vary according to the pace of democratic transformation, the structure of ruling elites, its openness to external influence, the society's demand for more efficient police, and other factors dealing with the unique political development of any given country.

In the context of former Soviet states, police reform typically seeks at least one of three outcomes. First, a police reform agenda entails disbanding institutions of oppression that allowed the former political leadership to use the police to protect themselves from the allegedly unruly masses. Instead of being used as a punitive instrument of oppression, the police learn to behave in transparent, accountable ways. Ideally, the post-Soviet police begin to work on behalf of the public, not the regime, and act by the law, not government orders.[9] The police abandon torture in favor of investigation and treat each citizen equally and fairly. The police uphold the law rather than merely enforce civilian obedience. This model of police reform therefore depends on the political liberalization of an ex-Soviet state.

Second, in the ex-Union of Soviet Socialist Republic (USSR), police reform implies a process in which the government and society establish control over an unruly element—be that an insurgent group, corrupt officials, or organized criminal group—that sprang from the collapse of the centrally planned economy. Two decades of poor policing, rampant corruption, and weak state structures encouraged and solidified the activity of such violent nonstate groups. At times, these groups become providers of alternative security by protecting criminals and corrupt politicians.[10] This unruly mass refuses to obey state regulations, instead working to ensure that state policies are designed to favor their business interests and further undermine state authority. In the cases of Georgia and Kyrgyzstan, like many ex-Soviet states, this often means eradicating the link between state actors and criminals, connections forged mainly in the waning years of the USSR.[11]

Finally, police reform means giving the newly liberalized society control over the police forces, entrusting the citizenry to police the police. It precludes forming new institutions and forms of interaction between society and the police. In short, the Interior Ministry must become responsive to citizens' concerns. In this sense, there are parts of Russia, Belarus, Uzbekistan, and Turkmenistan where not only has such a shift not taken place, but the deteriorating post-Soviet police forces have, in fact, amplified the police control over citizens. The police in these areas not only resort to the worst authoritarian practices, they also have become deeply politicized and corrupt.

With these arguments in mind, this report demonstrates that police reform is part of the larger process of redefining the functions of the state to reflect social and political changes. It includes dissolving old institutions, creating new ones, changing laws, and introducing new, pertinent policies. The decision to launch police reform almost uniformly comes as a response to a changing society and the emergence of new, nonstate threats. Tajikistan's President Emomali Rakhmon, for instance, became interested in police reform after a series of guerrilla attacks swept the

Rasht Valley in 2008 and 2009.[12] The Russian government started reform after public discontent with the police soared in the early-2000s.[13] Kazakhstan's government pledged to overhaul the Interior Ministry only after police shot dead 16 protestors in Zhanaozen town during the December 2011 riots there.[14]

In the post-Soviet reality, however, even creating a viable reform strategy is a significant challenge. The government must learn how to be open to input from both the public and the parliament, and to consider the opinions and experiences of both civilian and military officials. In countries where the government has little experience in collaborating with civil society or where the parliament is controlled by the ruling elites, the strategy can be usurped by political leaders, leaving little room for input from civic actors. At the same time, post-Soviet elites often fail to design a long-term, comprehensive strategy that clarifies the need for and benefits of police reform. Instead, they launch a series of expensive, often overlapping, changes.

Furthermore, attempts to design a comprehensive strategy are hindered by patronage networks linking law enforcement structures and political leaders. Police reform strategies almost always presume that personnel unable to meet the new standards of service will be removed and a new generation of police officers trained to take their place. This understanding makes Interior Ministry officials wary of reform, and they may merely pretend to enact reform in response to public criticism. Kyrgyzstan, where patronage networks between political leaders and Interior Ministry officials are strong, is a prime example of such anti-reform dynamics.

At the same time, the greater openness that law-enforcement structures show toward civil society while conducting the reform, the stronger will be the criticism of their previous practices. In Kyrgyzstan, Interior Ministry officials have tried to build a dialogue with civil society activists and a parliamentary committee dealing with law enforcement issues. But this collaboration has been rife with distrust and mutual accusations. In 2010-11, the political leadership invited leading NGO activists to participate in public forums to reflect upon the work of the Interior Ministry. The criticism aired at these events presented the Interior Ministry leadership as violators of basic human rights enmeshed in widespread corruption.

In Georgia, however, where reform was conducted during 2004-12 without public debate or civil society oversight, the police were not publicly attacked. The course of the reform reflected the will and vision of top political leadership seeking to meet expectations of the general public to clean up corruption after the Rose Revolution. Georgia's record, as will be discussed later, suggests that police reforms carried out without public participation always run the risk of serving the needs of authoritarian leaders, regardless of whether the police have been trained to respect human rights.

Furthermore, any reform effort must strike a balance among better procurement of equipment and supplies, improved service, and greater respect for human rights. There is an inherent danger that a reformed, better equipped, and more efficient police will actually strengthen government control over society. It is, therefore, vital that a police reform program reflects not only the government's strategic plan or the international community's recommendation, but it must also be the product of social deliberation.

Often the ex-Soviet states face pressure from the international community to remedy the human rights situation long before police professionalism and procurement is improved. Post-Soviet Interior Ministry officials, as well as political leaders, do not understand why human rights should be considered when dealing with individuals who may have committed serious crimes such as homicide or acts of terrorism. Police frequently use torture to extract evidence or elicit confessions because of the perception by police that criminals deserve harsh treatment.[15] Likewise, police officers justify brutality when they are faced with aggressive mobs and armed individuals. Human rights are considered to be an irrelevant, Western concept, and the police equate reform with losing these valuable tactics and placing themselves in danger.

To a large extent, post-Soviet police officers are quick to ignore the rights of citizens because their own rights are disrespected both by political leaders and society. As with other public employees in the post-Soviet space, they receive low wages, little training, and do not have the equipment and technology needed to carry out their duties. Public distrust of public employees goes far beyond just the police; it also applies to teachers, doctors, tax collectors, etc. The only difference between those public servants and the police is that the latter carry weapons and are authorized to use violence.

One common feature of post-Soviet police forces is a high rate of violence on the job.[16] Because citizens believe the police regularly use harsh physical violence against suspects, they tend to approach police officers with aggression and hostility. This generates cycles of violence between corrupt police and the civilian population that distrusts the police. Statistics suggest that the fears are justified on both sides. With the rise of illicit nonstate activity, including organized criminal groups, paramilitary groups, and mafia in the post-Soviet era, the rate of violence between police and public has further increased. Society does not trust the police to perform their function properly, and the police are unable to enforce state regulation of society without violence. Instead, the police are seen as representatives of the state who are allowed to persecute ordinary citizens, extort bribes, and protect the real criminals.[17]

GEORGIA

Georgia is a unique example of rapid police reform engendered by broader political change. President Saakashvili came to power through the bloodless Rose Revolution in 2003, which launched a series of sweeping reforms in Georgia. Together with a small group of close confidants, Saakashvili pushed forward a broad range of reforms that have made Georgia one of the most Westernized post-Soviet states.[18] During the earliest days of his presidency, he decided to begin reform with the patrol police—the highly visible police officer would embody the immediate results of his fight against corruption.[19] The foremost goal was to curb the petty corruption plaguing virtually every encounter between ordinary citizens and the police.

By 2006, such petty corruption had been virtually eradicated while the Interior Ministry has made great strides to boost its transparency and efficiency.[20] Crime rates dropped, and, in a dramatic shift, the police have become one of the most trusted public institutions in the country. Georgia's reformed police and public administration, as well as drastically reduced crime rates, have helped make state services more efficient and available to all citizens.[21]

The rapid transformation of the police is particularly impressive, given that in the early-2000s, Georgia's police was perhaps among the worst force in the entire former Soviet space. The police extorted bribes reaching $20,000-$30,000 per favor and turned to drug dealing to make ends meet. A promotion in the Interior Ministry costs anywhere between $2,000 and $20,000, depending on where it fell in seniority.[22] The corruption scheme was essentially pyramid shaped, with the top leaders getting a cut from all levels below. Most encounters with the police ended up with citizens bribing the police to not file charges. Organized criminal groups often received police protection from other state institutions. The country's police became a symbol of the failing Georgian state, one in which the government is not only not accountable to the citizens, it actually preys on society by expropriating revenues from licit and illicit sources. Corrupt police, controlled by criminals and uninterested in maintaining public safety, became one of the greatest points of public dissatisfaction with President Eduard Shevarnadze's regime in the 1990s and early-2000s.[23]

A closer look, however, reveals that Georgia's fast-paced reform has its weaknesses.[24] Powerful state officials imposed reform from above, not bothering with public accountability or debate. Although the parliament is formally charged with controlling the Interior Ministry, in reality police reform has always been a collaboration between the interior minister and the president. Post-reform, parliamentary oversight of the Interior Ministry's work remains weak, and the Interior Ministry has arguably become the most powerful structure in the country. The interior minister, who must have a civilian background, takes both strategic and operational decisions without public input or parliamentary oversight.[25] The interior minister, in effect, has the right to order the use of force in any given situation. This sweeping power is likely to change following the October 1, 2012, parliamentary elections, in which the opposition coalition, Georgian Dream, gained 55 percent of the vote. With a broader spectrum of political forces in the new parliament and government, the debate over the future course of police reform is likely to be intense. The new government faces the challenge of ensuring that the police is depoliticized and does not serve the interests of one political leader or faction, while also preserving its image as an efficient and uncorrupt institution.

The Reform.

Georgia's police reform was launched under Shevarnadze's presidency in the early-2000s. It followed a path similar to that of other former Soviet states—a few minor changes were made in police operations with the help of the international community. Shevarnadze was able to secure ample democracy-funding packages by Western donors.[26] Most initiatives failed to decrease corruption inside the Interior Ministry, and regime members remained reluctant to break their ties with organized criminal groups. According to former Interior Ministry press-secretary Shota Utiashvili, Shevardnadze tried to crack-down on criminal leaders, only to use their services during elections.

Saakashvili's government took a radically different approach. The Interior Ministry was fundamentally restructured, becoming the largest government body by the mid-2000s. Sixteen former departments were placed under the umbrella of the ministry, including the Counter Intelligence Department, the Counter Terror Center, the Special Operative Department (SOD), the Constitutional Security Department (KUD), the Special Tasks Main Division, the General Inspections Bureau, the Criminal Police Department, the Security Police, the Border Police, the Police Academy, and the Ministry of Emergencies. According to government officials, there is now a strong checks and balances system among the departments.[27] The Interior Ministry has grown significantly in importance, while decreasing the number of uniformed security personnel. Before the merger, 65,000 people worked in the law enforcement system; today the ministry has 27,000 employees, including 4,000 border guards. The ratio of police officers per citizen has shrunk from 1:21 to 1:89.[28]

Known for his excellent leadership skills, Ivane (Vano) Merabishvili headed Georgia's Interior Ministry between December 2004 and July 2012. However, his formal and informal duties went far beyond those of a typical interior minister. Throughout his tenure at the Interior Ministry, Merabishvili was widely regarded as one of the most powerful public officials in Georgia, and he advised Saakashvili on domestic and regional security issues.[29] Formally, Saakashvili entrusted the minister with absolute power over the course of police reform. Merabishvili's authority and managerial skills meant that policy decisions regarding police reform were executed quickly, encountering little opposition from the lower ranks of bureaucrats and police officers. Merabashvili was granted the Order of St. George for "heroism and courage in protection of the motherland and its unity" and contributions "to building independent Georgian statehood."

In July 2012 Saakashvili appointed Merabishvili as prime minister. He served in this position very briefly, as the ruling United National Movement party lost the parliamentary elections 3 months later.[30]

Although Merabishvili studied examples of successful police reform in other countries, Georgia's Interior Ministry reform was an ad hoc series of changes without any written or negotiated concept for short-term and long-term goals.[31] Various features of police functioning were borrowed from Estonia, Kosovo, and the United States. Italy's anti-mafia law and the U.S. Racketeer Influenced and Corrupt Organization (RICO) Act served as the basis for laws against organized crime.[32] The spontaneous nature of Georgia's reform effort has, nevertheless, led to visible results. Within a few years, the patrolman's mission has transformed from crime-focused operations into service providers who help society by carrying out the rule of law.[33] The police have learned the importance of respecting human rights in their everyday interaction with citizens. Off-the-record, one Interior Ministry official admitted that this change has been a pleasant and unexpected byproduct of the greater professionalism of police work as well as better procurement of equipment and supplies.[34]

The reform was essentially composed of four main dimensions: downsizing the police force and hiring new personnel, restructuring the Interior Ministry, boosting professionalism among rank-and-file personnel, and changing the procurement process.[35] Within the first 2 years, the government fired roughly 16,000 policemen.[36] Furthermore, most of the policemen who lost their jobs had been part of the *Gosudarstvennaya avtomobil'naya inpektsiya* (GAI) (a Soviet version of road militsiya), which was eliminated as part of the process of restructuring the ministry. In 2004, there was a period of about a month without any patrol police on the streets of Tbilisi before the new personnel were hired.

The reform aimed at breaking ties between the police and criminal groups. According to Utiashvili, the initial reaction was to just reduce the power of GAI personnel, many of whom were alleged to have strong ties with the criminal underground world. "But after some deliberation, the ministry came to a conclusion that all policemen were corrupt and realized that there is nothing we can change about them," he said. "So we retired them all in summer 2004."[37] The firing of police personnel proceeded gradually, yet the pace was fast enough to produce positive results within 2 months. After the reform was launched, about 500 police officers were arrested in 2 years for some type of illegal activity — taking bribes, having connections with criminal groups, and violating human rights. Of those, 90 percent were former police who had worked in the ministry before the reform.[38]

By 2012, the Interior Ministry described the Georgian patrol and community police as law abiding professionals who both obey and represent the law.[39] The contemporary image is a far cry from the earlier reputation for extorting bribes from the public. "Instead of old, fat policemen, people saw young lads well dressed and well equipped; instead of Zhiguly [cars], they saw VW," Utiashvili says. Refusing bribes is perhaps the most important professional code that new recruits must follow. "We told the new hires that we will give you good payment, uniform and require from them one thing — don't take bribes," Utiashvili recalls. Policemen interviewed for this report expressed high satisfaction with their job, saying they honor their professional mission to serve and protect ordinary citizens. Police personnel receive generous social benefits, including health insurance and a retirement plan.

Establishing transparency and increasing the Interior Ministry's capacity to execute its own misson were the reform's top priorities from the start. The Interior Ministry's headquarters are famously located in a new glass curtain-wall building, literally signifying the transparency of the public institution. By 2012, the majority of police stations across the country had been renovated to feature similar glass exteriors.[40] While the glass is used to signify transparency, the headquarters' grandiose design and estimated $500 million price tag also signify the government's sheer superiority over criminal leaders. "It is meant to show criminals that we are stronger than they are," one government official explained.[41] Police cars are equipped with portable computers, while every policeman carries a tablet computer listing legal statutes. Police also have ready access to a new database of all registered cars and drivers.

Perhaps the most impressive achievement of the reform has been the elimination of special treatment for government officials or politically well-connected individuals when detained for routine incidents such as drunk driving and traffic accidents. Such special treatment, when political officials are able to get away with crimes, is a common predicament across the former Soviet region.

Finally, the overhaul of the Police Academy became one of the reform's hallmarks. The Soviet-style 5-year curriculum was abandoned in favor of roughly 4 months of intensive training. New screening tests were introduced to select physically fit, educated men and women to join the law enforcement sector. Only candidates with BA or MA degrees may apply, because Interior Ministry officials believe that a university degree allows future police officers a better understanding of the nature of police work, including legal codes and concepts such as human rights.[42] Candidates must pass a written test and an interview with the academy's professors and psychologists.

Admission to the Police Academy is highly competitive. While in 2006 there were five applicants for each spot, in 2012 the number of candidates increased to 50 per spot. Female candidates comprise roughly 20 percent of all candidates, and 15 percent of them are accepted. After swearing into active duty, all officers are expected to be dedicated to their profession "because it is difficult, dangerous, routine, you deal with crazy people."[43] Most servicemen return for postgraduate specialized training twice a year. In order to receive a promotion, police officers must satisfactorily complete additional training courses and receive recommendations from the academy. By 2006, policemen's salaries had increased, and a standardized recruitment system was in place. The Police Academy's head is specifically chosen from a civilian background, so they may bring new ideas for further improvements in the curriculum.

The reform reinforced Saakashvili's popularity at home and abroad, becoming the signature component of his reform agenda and political will. According to one former Interior Ministry official, Saakashvili was very lucky to have early results from his rapid anti-corruption reform, because it would have been much more difficult to conduct it later in his presidency. The "euphoria and optimism" that accompanied the Rose Revolution greatly facilitated public support for the reforms.[44]

At the reform's outset, the Interior Ministry consulted with international donors. However, Georgian officials insist that external actors did not play any substantial role in guiding the reform process, and that most initiatives were internally generated. Government officials also deny that donor funds played any substantial role, insisting that financial resources were sought locally. They argue that the new post-Shevardnadze government created a special development fund to finance reforms using domestic donors.[45] Cleaning up corruption and legalizing the shadow economy helped Saakashvili's government to collect more taxes, which were then spent on additional reforms. International funds were mostly used to maintain the country's financial stability. Indeed, Georgia's gross domestic product (GDP) grew at 9 percent in 2004, largely as a result of legalizing the shadow economy.[46]

Furthermore, Georgian NGOs argue that Saakashvili's government generated a stream of funds through plea bargain deals in which former members of Shevarnadze's government agreed to invest in the development fund in return for having corruption charges against them dropped.[47] Finally, some members of the political opposition argue that, when still aligned with President Saakashvili, billionaire Bidzina Ivanishvili invested $600 million in various government projects, including the police reform.[48]

While Saakashvili's government was determined to find the right formula to transform its police, its reform efforts were still bankrolled by generous foreign aid. Between 1993 and 2010, Georgia received a total of $3.37 billion in U.S. aid. At least $1 billion of this amount was provided in the wake of the Rose Revolution in 2003. Following the August 2008 war with Russia, the U.S. Government pledged another $1 billion in humanitarian aid and reconstruction assistance, reinforcing Washington's position as the country's largest single donor.[49] Starting in 2002, the United States trained and equipped members of the Georgian armed forces so they could participate in Operation ENDURING FREEDOM and the U.S.-led Multinational Force-Iraq.[50] In addition, the Millennium Challenge Corporation, a private U.S. Government foreign aid agency, allocated $395 million for the period 2006-11. These funds were used to rebuild roads, water and energy systems, and the agricultural sector.[51] Altogether, this makes Georgia one of the highest recipients of U.S. aid on a per capita basis.

When reforms began, the international community was skeptical about the initiative. However, the reform process proceeded so swiftly that international donor organizations did not have time to formulate their own assessment. Instead, they had to rely on reports from the Georgian government.[52] By 2010, the police reform had become a symbol of Georgia's modern statehood, earning generous praise from the international community. For instance, one World Bank report gave the following qualitative, rather than analytical, assessment:

> The government viewed its strong-handed approach toward establishing law and order as essential to making people think differently, destroying respect toward the criminal underworld, and demonstrating the authority of formal legal institutions over informal ones.[53]

Likewise, a popular book by Larisa Burakova, *Pochemu u Gruzii poluchilos'?* (Why did Georgia Make It?), argues that the fact that public support in the police remains so high and the crime rate so low testifies to the reform's success.[54] She further claims that, to date, regime critics have yet to uncover a single corruption scheme among the Saakashvili-era higher political leaders.[55] The Saakashvili administration enthusiastically endorsed both the book and the World Bank's report.

In May 2011, Saakashvili said that police reform was the "first reform we carried out and remains the first symbol of our transformation and the creation of our new statehood."[56] He added:

> The main difference is that the Soviet *militsia* considered people [as if they were] their property and objects of humiliation, extortion and torture. Today's police consider that they belong to the people, [they] represent, protect, and serve them. That's why people respond with love. You feel it in your job, your family members feel it in everyday life.

Saakashvili further compared the achievements in police reforms with Georgia's most powerful historic symbols of statehood:

> We have managed to create a modern statehood. This is the historic legacy of the current generation, which will live on for the next 10 centuries, like it has remained in our history that [Georgian King] David the Builder [1089-1125] managed to do the same 10 centuries ago.[57]

The president sees the reform as a phase leading to Georgia's further Westernization and Europeanization.[58]

A "Police State."

The positive reputation of Georgia's neighborhood patrolman has reinforced similar positive images of the police and the Interior Ministry in general.[59] Importantly, however, such evenhanded, service-oriented treatment of all citizens is merely the standard operating procedure for trivial, everyday public interaction with the police. The transformation of the law enforcement sector did not curb corruption at the highest levels, among top officials who have access to economic resources.[60] It is difficult for the general public to understand what is really happening within the Interior Ministry.[61] Unless an individual openly supports the opposition or has relatives who do so, the population at large has no interaction with the politicized sectors of the Interior Ministry.

Formally, Interior Ministry staff are not allowed to intervene in the political process or even be members of a political party. But the quick reform generated by the political leadership has inevitably led to the politicization of the Interior Ministry. Under Merabishvili's leadership, the ministry often promoted police personnel based on their individual loyalty to the political leadership, not their skills or professionalism. In many rural areas, local police chiefs enjoy strong political power on par with local government officials.

Furthermore, the Police Academy still lacks a robust human resources system that would prevent promotion based on patronage networks.[62] According to the Transparency International office in Georgia, the international community has pressed the Interior Ministry to improve human resource management, but this recommendation was never implemented. "They prefer to have loyal people rather than professionals," one technical information (TI) expert said.[63]

Finally, the police reform model is now being applied to other institutions. Encouraged by the apparently successful reform of the police, the government has been using the Police Academy to train security guards for other government agencies, including the Ministry of Education.[64] Although those employees have civilian status, they are trained within the premises of the Interior Ministry.

Saakashvili's opponents insist that Georgia has essentially turned into a "police state" where the Interior Ministry spies on regime opponents. As a former opposition leader, Georgia's Defense Minister Irakli Alasania argues that before October 2012 elections, the Constitutional Security Department (KUD) regularly wiretaped phone numbers belonging to him, members of his family, and members of his political party. He also claims that the Interior Ministry's undercover representatives follow him whenever he meets with his constituents. The KUD also has "limitless power to investigate" the work of the political opposition, Alasania claims. Conveniently, ministry officials are immune to prosecution in cases when they break the law when dealing with the opposition.

The ministry's pervasive oversight of the opposition's activities undermined opposition parties' ability to campaign effectively and freely. In the run-up to the election, Bidzina Ivanishvili, then leader of the Georgian Dream coalition, openly alleged that the police are loyal to the regime and protect the president by engaging in illegal activities against his opponents.[65] Ivanishvili claimed the police were on standby to carry out politically motivated orders against opposition forces. In one incident, the police seized 300,000 satellite television dishes distributed to the population to help them access pro-opposition TV channels.[66] Opposition leaders further complained that their relatives were constantly harassed and threatened with arrest.

The government critics' main concern is Saakashvili's "zero-tolerance" policy toward corruption and criminal charges, meaning that anyone suspected of corruption is subject to prosecution. Merabishvili and former Justice Minister Zurab Adeishvili have been the primary masterminds behind the policy, which since the Rose Revolution has caused Georgia's prison population to reach 24,244 in 2012, compared to 6,654 in 2004.[67] The government publicizes arrests of criminals and politicians suspected of corruption on TV, demonstrating their own resolve to prosecute anyone not complying with the law. There have been cases when political figures were publicly accused of corruption without having a proper trial.[68] Multiple reports suggest that plea bargain funds are used to finance the state budget to such a degree that the judicial system almost entirely depends on this income.[69] Georgia's Ombudsman's office insists that, now that the level of petty corruption crimes has dramatically decreased, the government's zero-tolerance policy should end as well.[70]

The Georgian Public Defender's office is also concerned about police officers who still use excessive force or intentionally drag out criminal investigations. The Ombudsman's office has detected several cases of police restricting detainees' access to family members and not documenting cases of arrests. Police officers still often use excessive force during detention, and investigators are aware of several cases of inhumane treatment. Finally, Georgia's Public Defender argues that police detain citizens without cause to interrogate them on their activities.

Dealing with Mass Riots.

Georgian police's response to mass demonstrations in 2007, 2009, 2011, and 2012 has evolved as well. Before the November 2007 riots, when opposition leaders from the National Council gathered over 50,000 people to demonstrate in Tbilisi against Saakashvili's corruption, the Interior Ministry had only 600-700 policemen trained to deal with large crowds. Unprepared and ill-trained, the policemen resorted to fist fighting and excessive violence to subdue the protestors.[71] The protests lasted for several days before being dispersed by tear gas and water cannons. The police were widely criticized by human rights organizations for their brutal suppression of civilian demonstrations.[72]

Since the 2007 protests, the Interior Ministry has increased the number of trained riot police, now estimated at 5,000 men, many of whom serve in various police units. The government was better prepared for protests that took place in May 2011 when roughly 10,000 people walked the streets together with the Democratic Movement-United Georgia movement led by former prime minister Nino Burjanadze. The opposition blamed the police forces for brutally suppressing the demonstrations, in which two protesters died, accusing the police of acting unprofessionally. The government denied such reports, instead blaming the opposition for poor crowd management. While the government and opposition accounts of police actions differed, the Ombudsman's office determined that police did use excessive force against demonstrators.

Both the government and opposition forces condemn some of the police's violent treatment of demonstrators during mass protests in Tbilisi, Kalheti, and other parts of Georgia. However, whereas the government argues that the police were not prepared to handle mass protests and that some opposition leaders were guilty of initiating violence, nongovernmental actors regard the actions by the police as confirmation of their willingness to support Saakashvili's regime at the cost of the welfare of the masses.

NGOs have collected complaints that participants of mass demonstrations received threatening phone calls during the demonstrations.[73] The Georgian Young Lawyers Association (GYLA) reports that policemen openly expressed their support of the president by shouting his name during the 2011 protests. Policemen were spotted accusing the crowds of being Russian spies paid by Moscow to stage the rallies. In situations like this, the police have shown that "they are not the protector of people, but they protect the regime," GYLA executive director Ekaterine Popkhadze said.[74] Those arrested during mass protests undergo unfair trials conducted by a politicized judiciary.[75] Even minor, small-scale protests result in arrests.

Saakashvili's strong political will is a common explanation for the fast-paced reforms of the police and other government sectors.[76] However, the Georgian example demonstrates that political will can look a great deal like personal power grabs to ensure continuity. Georgia's case also vividly demonstrates that the public perception of corruption depends highly on the visibility of corruption at the grassroots levels. Once petty corruption is eliminated, the population believes the political regime is carrying out similar anti-corruption fights across the board.[77]

Yet, because the reform was conducted without public oversight, public suspicion about high-level corruption in the Interior Ministry continues to mount. Just 2 weeks before the October 1, 2012, parliamentary election, videos appearing to document cases of torture and rape in Gldani prison in Tbilisi were leaked to the Internet, raising widespread concerns about human rights abuses in detention facilities. The video showed prisoners, some of them underage, beaten, raped, and forced to confess by prison guards.[78] The videos triggered spontaneous anti-government rallies across Georgia. Newly appointed Interior Minister Bacho Akhalia and prison officials were forced to resign. The videos may have affected the final outcome of the elections and helped cause Saakashvili's party to lose its majority in the parliament.

KYRGYZSTAN

Ten years into the effort to reform Kyrgyzstan's police, corruption is still pervasive at the Interior Ministry, which has become infamous for widespread human rights abuses. Although some minor changes to police operations were introduced over the past decade, such as elements of community policing and using rubber bullets to disperse protestors, these changes are dwarfed by the increase in some of the worst Soviet legacies: forced confessions, petty graft, and police readiness to serve the political regime at the expense of society. At best, the police are considered to be inefficient at maintaining social order, at worst, they are a source of injustice and a threat to public security. In most rural areas, police are afraid of local organized criminal groups and limit their own contacts with society.[79]

Kyrgyz human rights activists have uncovered 20 cases of police torture that led to the death of detainees from 2008 to 2011. Not all instances of police misconduct are reported, and various forms of torture and coercion are commonly used by cops to extract evidence and confessions.[80] The situation is even murkier in southern Kyrgyzstan. In the June 2010 bloodshed in Osh, the police and armed forces joined the conflict, rather rather than resolving it. They acted unprofessionally and reportedly provoked the Uzbek minority and protected the Kyrgyz majority. Their lack of adequate training to deal with ethnic-driven civic unrest and the shortage of equipment exacerbated the problem.

For the most part, Kyrgyzstan's Interior Ministry preserved the Soviet institutional foundations of law enforcement, including the ministry's Soviet-era departments, mission statement, and educational system. Policemen spend 5 years training at the Police Academy, yet they remain the least respected professionals in society. Corruption and abuse of power begins the day after a cadet graduates from the Police Academy.[81] In summer 2011, to celebrate their graduation, new policemen in uniforms blocked an intersection in central Bishkek and openly drank vodka disregarding traffic jams caused by them. In 2012 they started a massive brawl in one of Bishkek cafes, destroying private property and ignoring warnings from their Interior Ministry superiors to stop.[82]

When the Organization for Security and Cooperation in Europe (OSCE) first began collaborating with the Kyrgyz government in 2002 to implement a 10-year police reform program, the organization sought to make Kyrgyzstan a model case for police reforms in other post-communist countries.[83] Together with the Kyrgyz government, the OSCE developed a long-term strategy that would change the structure of the police, making it accountable to the population, not political leaders. Kosovo's successful police reform in the early-2000s has served as an inspiration for the OSCE office in Bishkek.[84]

The most common criticism is that the OSCE tried to apply other international experiences in Kyrgyzstan without trying to understand the local context. Some of the attempts at collaboration between, for example, Georgian and Turkish experts and their Kyrgyz counterparts brought little result. International donors did not fully understand the basic patterns of interaction between society and police before doling out advice to the Kyrgyz authorities. Instead, donors used their existing playbook, prescribing reforms that worked in other countries and relied on gossip and chitchat about how the local Interior Ministry works.[85]

Throughout the 2000s, the Kyrgyz government continued to push police reform despite growing authoritarianism under both the Askar Akayev and Kurmanbek Bakiyev regimes. The OSCE prioritized its reform assistance efforts on developing police capacity to fight transnational threats such as terrorism, drug trafficking, and organized crime. Still, most of OSCE projects were ad hoc, not following any coherent strategy.[86] International donors have also helped Kyrgyzstan's police forces to become better skilled at peacefully dispersing mass riots.[87] Civil society activists, however, depicted the Akayev-OSCE collaboration as a case of the international community helping a corrupt, authoritarian regime to more effectively suppress civilian protests and opposition groups.

As the international community's interest in Kyrgzstan's attempts at police reform continued, a group of high-ranking Interior Ministry officials became gatekeepers, accepting donor funds on behalf of the ministry, but were more interested in keeping the money channel open than conducting any reform.[88] By 2011, these gatekeepers blamed Akayev and Bakiyev for failing to overhaul the police and continued to request greater and greater financial assistance to try "real reform" now that these obstructions were out of the picture. Corruption among Interior Ministry officials and political leaders has stalled any effort to reform the police, but it also helped the Interior Ministry to continue functioning when its official budget shrank in the 1990s.[89] With their own source of "independent" funding, the Interior Ministry and the police became increasingly detached from both state and society. The police became a separate marketplace funded through graft, organized crime, and extortion.[90] Hence, the Interior Ministry does not need to depend on state funding or civilian oversight.

Police reform in Kyrgyzstan was further slowed by the chaotic political situation. Two regime changes within 5 years (March 2005 and April 2010), coupled with rotation among the OSCE staff in Bishkek, have forced the reform into a reset mode, resulting in many repetitive and redundant activities. Since most of the OSCE representatives dealing with the reform spent between 2 and 4 years in Kyrgyzstan, Kyrgyz Interior Ministry officials often intentionally stalled the reform effort. At the same time, Kyrgyz NGOs preferred to see large-scale, long-term, and well-funded police reform projects. The Interior Ministry, on the other hand, defends its limited progress, complaining that international donors expect the police to respect human rights under conditions in which law enforcement agencies in relatively underdeveloped countries still use paper to communicate between agencies and across different parts of the country.

Kyrgyzstan's experience demonstrates that international pressure can make it relatively easy for Interior Ministry officials to adopt policies, but it may not be sufficient reason to trigger genuine institutional change. Much of the criticism from the expert community centered to the fact that international assistance usually meant providing better equipment, not implementing structural reforms.[91] As a result, over the years the better-equipped police became a more efficient instrument of repression in the hands of authoritarian leaders.

Kyrgyzstan's case thus shows that external pressure and financial aid alone will not lead to a thorough police reform. OSCE representatives, as well as U.S. and European Union (EU) donors understated the Kyrgyz leadership's reluctance to transform the police forces to serve the interests of the broader population. Like Georgia, Kyrgyzstan has received ample U.S. aid over the past 2 decades. Between 1992 and 2010, the United States provided aid packages that totaled $1.22 billion.[92] This includes $90 million in humanitarian assistance allocated following the regime change and ethnic violence in 2010. Since late-2001, Kyrgyzstan has also received U.S. payments for rent and costs associated with the U.S. air base (Transit Center) at the Manas airport. Bakiyev. Later President Almazbek Atambayev secured up to $150 million in annual payments for use of the base, with at least $100 million earmarked for rent.[93] U.S. humanitarian programs associated with the Transit Center had spent $1.7 million by 2010.

Reform Programs and Authoritarian Leadership.

President Askar Akayev became interested in police reform in March 2002, following an unprecedented incident in which police shot at civilian demonstrators, killing six. The OSCE was quick to respond to Akayev's pleas for assistance in transforming the country's police forces. Akayev's initiative with the OSCE, however, encountered strong resistance from civil society activists. Kyrgyz NGOs warned that Akayev, whose popularity was rapidly sinking due to pervasive corruption, would use a more professional police force to suppress his opponents more efficiently.

Nevertheless, in August 2003, the OSCE and the Kyrgyz government signed a Memorandum of Understanding on transforming the Interior Ministry.[94] This marked the beginning of the restructuring program, which identified critical areas: improving the quality of investigations conducted, strengthening the forces and means to curb drug trafficking, creating service centers for emergency calls, strengthening the capacity of law enforcement bodies for conflict prevention and peaceful resolution of social unrest, and implementing pilot projects in community-based policing in Bishkek.

Under the Memorandum, the OSCE would help the Interior Ministry to develop a community-based system that would meet international standards of policing. International experts were invited to train Interior Ministry personnel, while Kyrgyz officials could participate in courses abroad. Between 2003-08, roughly 4,000 Interior Ministry employees were trained under the banner of the OSCE reform program. In addition, the ministry received 88 vehicles and roughly 200 computer stations, and five training centers were established within the ministry's academy. Within the OSCE's more narrowly targeted Police Assistance Program (PAP), Kyrgyzstan's police received new computers, over 800 surplus hand-held radios, and specialized vehicles with crime-scene equipment.[95] OSCE introduced the concept of community policing early on, but years passed before it spread throughout Bishkek and then the country at large.

Other projects were created to improve the professionalism of ministry personnel, such as strengthening the capacity of the Chief of Staff of the Ministry of the Interior to monitor the activities of all units, analyzing decisionmaking processes, and improving psychological counseling for ministry personnel. Furthermore, 10 projects were developed specifically for the Police Academy, including establishing a research institute within the ministry. To improve the work of community-based policing, the Interior Ministry planned to improve investigative units, forensic departments, the emergency call center, and analytical services; upgrade crime labs; and implement targeted programs to prevent crime, religious extremism, juvenile delinquency, livestock theft in rural areas, and domestic violence.

By 2008, when Akayev's successor, Kurmanbek Bakiyev, organized rigged parliamentary elections and significantly limited media freedom, police reform stalled. By then, mass protests were banned, and Bakiyev had built a robust security apparatus to protect him from his opponents. Law enforcement agencies and security institutions became highly politicized. Bakiyev appointed cronies—individuals who valued political loyalty over professional qualifications—to head all power ministries, including the Interior Ministry.[96] The Soviet-inherited ranking system inside the Interior Ministry was disrupted, with many professionals leaving the ministry and those ready to support the regime unconditionally moving into higher ranks. Nevertheless, the OSCE continued to fund the reform under Bakiyev's regime.

In March 2008, the Interior Ministry and the OSCE began to improve the legal framework for police operations, data collection and legal support, human resource capacity and the ministry press office, the ministry's education system, and the work of criminal investigators and community police, and worked to introduce principles of international law into the national legal code.[97] During 2008-10, a special emphasis was made on improving information sharing, both within the ministry and between the ministry and citizens. According to the plan, the ministry would set up an online database containing key ministry documents as well as biometric data to improve searches based on the physical characteristics of suspects.[98]

The OSCE and other international donor efforts to overhaul Kyrgyzstan's police during 2002-12 largely failed to bring about changes in institutional practices and attitudes. Shamshybek Mamyrov, deputy head of the Chief Administration for Legal and Criminal Analysis at the Interior Ministry since the late 1990s, attributed the failure to what he described as "double standards" employed by former presidents Akayev and Bakiyev: the two leaders wanted police to improve professionalism in their ranks without trying to clean up corruption at the highest echelons of power.[99] In addition, politicians during the Akayev and Bakiyev eras frequently used law enforcement agencies to promote their personal agendas, not necessarily to uphold the law. Mamyrov, however, is often criticized for intentionally stalling the reform as the ministry's "gatekeeper" for international donors.

Reports of police misconduct have continued shortly after Bakiyev's regime crumbled. For example, the police failed to prevent looters from acquiring weapons during the violent regime change in

April 2010.[100] As happened during the regime change in March 2005, police forces in Bishkek stopped functioning immediately following the collapse of the government. This led to several days of looting and arson, forcing the population to organize their own civilian security units. Law enforcement officials have been accused of collaborating with criminal groups and of selectively targeting minorities during the June 2010 ethnic violence in southern Kyrgyzstan. There were also ongoing reports in southern Kyrgyzstan of police involvement in torture, unwarranted arrests, and the harassment of ethnic Uzbeks.

Moving the Reform Out of the Interior Ministry.

After the regime change in 2010, police reform has once again become the cornerstone of the Kyrgyz government's effort to boost public trust in the new regime. As prime minister and later as president, Atambayev has preferred to outsource responsibility for the reform to the Interior Ministry, NGOs, and MPs. The Interior Ministry opted to begin the post-2010 reform effort by changing laws and regulations.

Shortly after Bakiyev's fall in April 2010, the Interior Ministry formulated a reform concept that offered nothing new; instead, it merely changed some laws and increased salaries for police personnel. It lacked a conceptual base that explained why new laws were needed and described in what ways police would be different after the transformation. At the insistence of the OSCE's Vienna office, Mamyrov agreed to formulate a concept for the draft laws put forward after the regime change.[101] But ethnic violence in southern Kyrgyzstan in June 2010 and parliamentary elections in October 2010 postponed discussion of reform for another year.

Starting in 2011, Kyrgyz NGOs have shown increased interest in the reform effort, largely criticizing the Interior Ministry's lack of progress. The OSCE welcomed the involvement of NGO experts in designing police reform despite resistance from ministry officials. Coordinating the work of multiple NGOs was a complex process in itself. Members of NGOs, in turn, insisted that the concept be widely discussed with society at large. Several NGO activists traveled across the country to talk to local groups about the reform. This exercise was not very helpful, as the activists discovered that the population had very limited understanding of what reform should entail.[102]

By mid-2011, a special Working Group comprised of MPs, government officials, and NGO activists was formed to define a vision for police reform. Together with OSCE representatives, the group regularly met to discuss the reform goals and desired outcomes. Often, members discussed the police reform programs in Georgia and the Baltic states. The meetings rarely produced specific recommended actions, while Interior Ministry officials tended to ignore recommendations from civil society or even other members of the Working Group.[103] In the summer of 2011, for example, the ministry launched a month-long pilot police patrol program in Bishkek. The ministry also unilaterally decided to install street cameras in Bishkek and other cities.

By mid-2012, the Working Group had formulated a joint police reform concept that included four main points: democratization, demilitarization, depoliticization, and technology procurement. The concept further suggested reorganizing the Interior Ministry into three departments: patrol police, detectives, and community policing. Some among the NGO community were driven by the Georgian example, borrowing heavily from their collaboration with Georgian government officials. When NGOs cited the Georgian precedent during Working Group discussions, it almost uniformly portrayed it in rosy terms, leaving no space for doubt or criticism.[104]

This positive evaluation coincided with the Atambayev government's decision to follow Georgia's example and to begin by transforming the traffic police. Former Deputy Prime Minister and former Interior Minister Shamil Atakhanov visited Georgia to observe their program and is leading the efforts to implement a similar program in Kyrgyzstan. He was able to secure 10 million soms ($220,000) for this program from the state budget. Atakhanov has declared that the reform effort's main goal is to boost public trust in the police by reducing corruption, unwarranted arrests, and the use of torture. The pilot project started in August 2011 and was suspended in October 2011 for the presidential election campaign and never resumed again.

It took roughly a year to develop the concept because Working Group members had to accommodate the desire of several NGOs to contribute their vision of the reform. At least two concept papers competed for attention, with NGOs, Interior Ministry, and government officials each suggesting their own vision. Since the perception in the parliament and government is that international donors are more likely to trust NGOs than state officials, all realized that civil society's participation in the creation and implementation of the concept was necessary.

Multiple voices within civil society competed over what type of concept to propose, delaying their endorsement of the document until mid-2012. Some

Interior Ministry officials viewed the battle for controlling policy formulation as a competition over potentially managing external grants and raising their personal profile inside the country.[105]

The bulk of the discussion centered on whether the reform should proceed gradually or rapidly. Advocates of gradualism spelled out stages for the reform and considered the Interior Ministry's vision for the process, while the latter insisted on laying off all police personnel and rehiring them again based on the results of testing.

Another major point of debate was how to manage property belonging to the ministry. The liberal-minded NGO Central Asia Free Market Institute (CAFMI) wanted to privatize resorts belonging to the ministry and increase salaries for personnel, while the leader of the human rights NGO "Nashe pravo," Kalicha Umuralieva, argued that it would not be possible to increase rank-and-file policemen's salaries to a level that would allow them to still afford vacations at similar resorts. That is, social benefits after the reform would not match pre-reform levels.

After months of debate, the NGOs came to a conclusion that instead of firing corrupt police personnel, the Interior Ministry will be restructured to decrease the number of nonpolice staff. This approach includes moving civilian personnel into the nongovernmental sector and using their services on a contract basis. In June 2012, Umuralieva predicted that up to 7,000 people would be downsized as part of the reform.[106] CAFMI, on the other hand, insisted that the reform must be conducted swiftly and, as in Georgia, all police personnel should be fired and made to pass exams if they want to regain their jobs.[107]

Nevertheless, by mid-2012, the concept was formulated after the locus of responsibility was moved out of the Interior Ministry to the Working Group that involved motivated NGO leaders, as well as MPs. The initiative for forming such a group originated in the NGO community and was supported by MPs and Prime Minister Babanov. The group also attracted police personnel who showed interest in the reform and were willing to convince their fellow colleagues. NGO representatives worked with the parliament and each MP individually, persuading them to support the concept. They chose to persuade, not criticize, in hopes of motivating MPs and Interior Ministry officials to move the reform forward.

The concept seeks to copy many elements of the Georgian reform, including reducing the training period to a few months and shutting down the 5-year programs at the Police Academy. Candidates now must have an undergraduate or graduate degree to be accepted. Community police and patrol police candidates are to take courses for a few weeks, while aspiring detectives will train for at least a year. This change is expected to significantly cut costs for training new conscripts. Under the old system, 600 students graduated from police training every year, but only 8 percent stayed within the Interior Ministry system, as the rest chose other career paths immediately after graduation.[108]

The concept paper's three fundamental principles are interpreted as follows:

- *Democratization* includes respect for human rights and collaboration with civil society-groups.[109]
- *Demilitarization* includes appointing a civilian minister and transforming the Interior

Ministry into a civilian agency. The new interior minister's efficiency will depend upon the level of public trust. Furthermore, under this clause, the concept suggests increasing police officers' salaries and introducing a bonus system for achievements beyond expectations. The concept suggests delinking the current bonus system from the number of cases solved by the policemen, instead rewarding their rapid deployment to crimes. Importantly, the ministry is to lay off 3,000 personnel in specialized units. Overall, the number of police personnel would decrease from 17,000 to 12,000.

- *Depoliticization* presumes detaching police forces from the political leadership. This would include preventing police forces from participation in political events and from harassing political figures.
- *Procurement* means improving the equipment and technology provided to police and opening new opportunities for continuing education within the Police Academy. As part of the reform a starting salary for the Interior Ministry personnel would more than double, to $400-600 per month.

According to MP Ravshan Jeenbekov, the Interior Ministry has agreed to implement the reform but is against the idea of appointing a civilian to head the police.[110] The ministry staff are also afraid that most of their benefits will be taken away in exchange for higher salaries. The MP alleges that the ministry's recreation centers, hospitals, and other state-funded facilities provide multiple opportunities for corruption. Most of the facilities were left over from the Soviet period, but the Interior Ministry later opened them to the broader population as a source of income.

Downsizing Interior Ministry personnel will be a challenging task for the government as well. The process inevitably increases tensions inside the parliament because some parties will lose control over public offices.[111] A number of high-ranking Interior Ministry personnel have strong ties with the criminal underworld and are not interested in changing how the ministry works.

The Policeman's Dilemma.

The police in Kyrgyzstan, like their colleagues in other former Soviet states, suffer from a negative image that is reinforced through the behavior of rank-and-file personnel in daily contact with society. They are seen as individuals willing to abuse their power, use violence against civilians, and collaborate with organized criminal groups. Some police officers openly admit that since most civilians disrespect them and are ready to break the law, they must themselves use their own judgment about what is "good" and "bad" when extorting bribes from the "bad" and "real criminals."[112] For others, this separation was not important, so they treat all violators of law as potential sources of bribes. Some policemen see their jobs primarily as fundraising for the Interior Ministry's higher leadership.[113]

This negative image is propped up by a network of informal relations within the Interior Ministry that reinforces corruption on all levels. In this system, the very top level of Interior Ministry personnel are very comfortable financially because the entire system works for them, as they reap returns from petty corruption in the lower ranks. Fresh graduates of the Police Academy earn meager salaries, or no salary at all, and are expected to collect petty bribes to meet informal requests for cash by their superiors. Moving up in the organization's hierarchy means gaining access to larger sums of informal income and lavish lifestyles, while promotions are distributed mostly according to a policeman's ability to bribe his superiors. As David Lewis describes a Central Asian example:

> Informal payments rapidly turned into a more formal parallel system of funding, in which money collected at the bottom of the force by ordinary police officers and traffic policemen was channeled up through the system to mid-level and high-level officers, with a final cut reserved for the minister, and in most cases, for his political masters.[114]

Indeed, once a policeman reaches the rank of minister, he achieves the rank of Police General and will enjoy generous state benefits for the rest of his life.[115]

In this system dominated by patronage relations rather than professional conduct, a small group of policemen are interested in reform as a way to gain the trust and respect of the population.[116] "My work is obsolete in this country," one policeman said. "I have a feeling of permanent injustice."[117] But these few individuals feel powerless to break the cycle of corruption maintained by their superiors. Furthermore, because the police are inefficient, alternative sources of justice and order have emerged throughout the country, arrangements that often sabotage the efforts of honest policemen. Organized crime, elders' courts, private security organizations, and corrupt policemen thrive in rural areas.

Most lower-ranking police personnel are therefore caught between an aggressive society wary of their work and corrupt leadership in the ministry and government. Ordinary rank-and-file police personnel often must decide whether they serve according to the formal mission of the police, survive on a low salary, and compete for professional promotion, or succumb to corruption and its unlimited opportunities for personal enrichment. Some police choose to cover up criminals instead of trying to make sense of their professional mission. They may structure their careers around opportunities for enrichment. For example, a narcotics squad officer in Issyk-Kul oblast in northern Kyrgyzstan might prefer to be relocated to Osh where drug routes offer more lucrative opportunities for bribes.[118] Similarly, most policemen prefer to work in larger cities rather than in rural areas because of the greater population density and concentration of wealth. Officers stationed in rural areas may seek to bribe their way into a transfer to a more populous area.

The Working Group has identified Interior Ministry officials and rank-and-file personnel interested in genuine reform and tried to involve them in the process so they might persuade their colleagues to accept the upcoming changes. MPs, however, complain that although some Interior Ministry members want to reform, they are thinking only within the limits of Kyrgyzstan's experience, without considering policies that have worked in other countries. "All they want to change is the structure, equipment, and salaries," Jeenbekov says. A group of NGO activists and MPs genuinely interested in the reform trusts neither the Interior Ministry nor the OSCE to move forward with the change. Their ability to push the reform past these obstacles will be revealed in the coming years.

By late-2012, Kyrgyzstan's new Interior Minister, Shamil Atakhanov, faced the challenge of implementing ideas developed by MPs and civil society leaders who were, in turn, inspired by the top-down police reform program in Georgia. The appointment of Atakhanov, a former Soviet police officer who more recently had spent 20 years in the civilian sector, was the government's first step toward implementing the Working Group's recommendations.

CONCLUSIONS AND RECOMMENDATIONS

Analyzing police reform in Georgia and Kyrgyzstan helps U.S. military engagement policymakers to better understand the challenges and opportunities that former Soviet republics face when reforming their security sectors. Both countries have made conscious attempts to build on existing democratic practices and to change the character of the militarized police inherited from the Soviet era. To date, however, external assistance programs have, at times, contributed to even greater political manipulation of the police. The politicization predicament is characteristic of the broader security sector in these countries, although the police are a unique component because they have direct contact with citizens.

Georgia and Kyrgyzstan present two different models of post-Soviet police reform. The major difference between the two cases is that Georgia vigorously carried out one man's vision using his substantial political skills and took advantage of the post-Rose Revolution "honeymoon" period. The government's reform program has fundamentally transformed the police, but it also reinforced the Saakashvili regime's reliance on the police. The larger question Georgia is facing today is whether the reformed police will retain their new efficiency at the grassroots level under the new government? More pertinent, how will the police react to public dissent under Georgia's newly split government?

After many starts and stops and regime changes in Kyrgyzstan, the pace of reform quickened only after several local NGOs inserted themselves in the process of designing and overseeing the reform in 2010-13. The future of the reform is still uncertain, but its concept has become a matter of broad public discussion with several activists and NGOs involved in the process. Small steps have been made toward implementing the reform in 2012.

Current and future U.S. military-to-military cooperation could potentially foster the transformation of the security sector in Central Asia and the South Caucasus. Surrounded by Russia and China, these regions are under constant pressure to broker military and security deals with Moscow and Beijing, deals that would hinder their democratic development. Particularly in Central Asia, where the EU is a marginal actor, U.S. military-to-military engagement could be beneficial.

Over the past decade, however, U.S. policy in Afghanistan has dominated the Pentagon's security sector programs with the Soviet successor states. The primacy of Afghanistan often trumped democratization efforts promoted by other U.S. Government agencies. To date, Central Asian and South Caucasus governments have readily accepted U.S. materiel and technical support as part of anti-terrorism efforts, but they have refrained from taking steps to increase public involvement in security sector oversight. The distance separating the security sector, including the police, from the civilian population remains as large as during the Soviet period.

To reverse this trend, the U.S. military must prioritize democratic security sector reform over improving a country's military technical capability. To do that, military-to-military assistance must focus on training and sharing best practices regarding civilian control of the armed forces, separation of military and police functions, and stripping the military of its political surveillance functions. A special panel/committee should be established to deal specifically with issues regarding the democratic reform of the security sector, and police reform must be part of that agenda. Technical assistance to Georgia and Kyrgyzstan, as well as other post-Soviet countries, must be provided only when indisputably democratic elements of security policy oversight are in place. Technical and material assistance provided by the U.S. military to post-Soviet counterparts must be transparent as well.[119]

Policymakers should expect government leaders in the former Soviet republics to resist demands for greater security sector transparency. While some of these states have appointed civilian Defense and Interior ministers, their security sectors remain exempt from external oversight. The U.S. European Command (EUCOM) and U.S. Central Command (CENTCOM) must consistently promote institutional reform to eliminate such political barriers and to enable fruitful military-to-military cooperation.

Greater security sector openness will help demilitarize the police, something police reform advocates throughout the former Soviet region have been promoting for the past several years. Georgia's experience confirms that trust in one security institution reinforces trust in other state institutions. That is, greater public trust in the police may potentially also boost public trust in the military. In turn, police forces that are able to maintain public order in a democratic way will reduce the potential need for military operations to counter nonstate challenges. Reformed police should be able to prevent violence generated by criminal syndicates, drug cartels, and violent entrepreneurs.

As part of these efforts, security sector efficiency must be evaluated according to criteria other than the technical sophistication of equipment and the number of military and police personnel. Instead, the Pentagon must assist efforts to expand the number of groups involved in public oversight of the security sector by bringing the parliament and NGOs into the process. Transformation of the security sector should be measured according to how transparent and accountable the military, police, and other components are becoming. Likewise, the success of programs to create interoperability between the Pentagon and security structures in Georgia and Kyrgyzstan should be measured by how well the shared vision of transparency and accountability of the military and police to civilian leadership and public oversight is implemented.

EUCOM and CENTCOM are therefore faced with the challenge of identifying which security sector actors are genuinely interested in creating greater transparency and institutional change, as well as identifying which civil society groups appreciate the urgent need to improve democratic control of the security sector. When possible, EUCOM and CENTCOM should prioritize the training of local military and police trainers and boost the participation of local experts to promote security sector reform. The Pentagon should also collaborate with local civilian experts to assess the security sector's democratization process. In Georgia particularly, EUCOM has a unique opportunity to engage both the President's office and members of the opposition in the process of depoliticizing the security sector and strengthening the sector's capacity to deal with state and nonstate threats, thanks to the broad consensus among competing political forces. Kyrgyzstan, where a number of civic activists have been engaged in the reform process, must be further encouraged to invest in building peace-keeping contingents that could undertake regional and international missions.

Finally, the Pentagon's security sector assistance program must strive for better synchronization with the democratization efforts of other agencies, including USAID and INL. This is particularly important, since countries like Georgia and Kyrgyzstan have shown interest in building on existing democratic practices. Assistance to transform the security sector in former Soviet states will, in the long term, build partners who will act in a more transparent way and prioritize security threats that affect the entire population, not just a narrow circle of political elites.

ENDNOTES

1. Arie Bloed, "The Slow Process of Police Reform in Central and Eastern Europe: Some Lessons Learned," Niels Uildriks, ed., *Police Reform and Human Rights: Opportunities and Impediments in Post-Communist Societies,* Cambridge, UK: Intersentia, 2005, pp. 35-39; Mark Galeotti, "Medvedev's Police Reform Is More About Control Than Reform," Radio Free Europe/Radio Liberty (RFE/RL), January 7, 2010, available from *www.rferl.org/content/Medvedevs_Police_Reform_Is_More_About_Control_Than_Reform/1923207.html.*

2. For more on political change in both countries, see Lincoln A. Mitchell, *The Color Revolutions,* Philadelphia, PA: University of Pennsylvania Press, 2012; Scott Radnitz, *Weapons of the Wealthy:*

Predatory Regimes and Elite-Led Protests in Central Asia, Ithaca, NY: Cornell University Press, 2012.

3. For more information, see the International Republican Institute's survey of public opinion in Georgia, January 5, 2012, available from *www.iri.org/news-events-press-center/news/iri-releases-expanded-nationwide-survey-georgian-public-opinion.*

4. According to the International Republican Institute's survey of public opinion in Kyrgyzstan, 59 percent of respondents viewed the police's work unfavorably in 2012, April 11, 2012, available from *www.iri.org/newsevents-press-center/news/iri-releases-post-presidential-election-survey-kyrgyzstan-public-opinion.*

5. See Data for 2005-11, "State/INL Georgia Program," December 6, 2011, available from *www.state.gov/j/inl/rls/fs/178347. htm.* Georgia was the largest INL aid recipient in the South Caucasus, compared to $21 million for the same time period in Armenia and $10.6 in Azerbaijan.

6. See Data for 2006-2011, December 6, 2011, "State/INL Kyrgyzstan Program," available from *www.state.gov/j/inl/rls/fs/ 178372. htm.* Likewise, Kyrgyzstan was the largest recipient of INL aid in Central Asia, compared to $1.7 million in Uzbekistan and $3 million in Turkmenistan. Tajikistan was the only country where INL spent more over the same time period - $46.3 million.

7. For more, see David H. Bayley, "Democratizing the Police Abroad: What to Do and How to Do It," *Issues in International Crime,* Washington, DC, 2001; Barry J. Ryan, *Statebuilding and Police Reform: The Freedom of Security,* London, UK: Routledge, 2011, pp. 50-54; Renate Weber, "Police Organization and Accountability: A Comparative Study," Andras Kadar, ed., *Police in Transition,* Budapest, Hungary: Central European University, 2001; David Alan Sklansky, *Democracy and the Police,* Stanford, CA: Stanford University Press, 2008.

8. Hans Toch, J. Douglas Grant, and Raymond T. Galvin, *Agents of Change: A Study in Police Reform,* New York: John Wiley & Sons, 1975; John Keane, *Violence and Democracy,* Cambridge, UK: Cambridge University Press, 2004.

9. Peter K. Manning, *Democratic Policing in a Changing World,* Boulder, CO: Paradigm Publishers, 2010, p. 13.

10. For more on state-crime relations in Georgia and Kyrgyzstan, see Alexander Kupatadze, *Organized Crime, Political Transitions, and State Formation in Post-Soviet Eurasia,* Basingstoke, Hampshire, UK: Palgrave Macmillan, 2012.

11. For more on violence and organized crime in former Soviet republics, see Vadim Volkov, *Violent Entrepreneurs: The Use of Force in the Making of Russian Capitalism,* Ithaca, NY: Cornell University Press, 2002.

12. "OSCE, Tajikistan to Sign MoU on Supporting Tajikistan's Police Forces," *Asia-Plus,* April 4, 2011.

13. Gilles Favarel-Garrigues's presentation, "Usual Suspect?: Police on Trial in Russia," at the Association for Slavic, East European, and Eurasian Studies (ASEEES), Pittsburgh, PA, November 20, 2011.

14. Opposition forces claim that the real number of casualties reached 50 people. A video report from Zhanaozen by "K Plus" TV channel, available from *www.youtube.com/watch?v=10wXcFu A6IQ&feature=share.*

15. See, for example, numerous reports by Human Rights Watch and Amnesty International, chapters on Uzbekistan and Kyrgyzstan in *Annual Report for 2012* by Amnesty International, New York; "Kyrgyzstan: Torture, Detentions Escalate Tensions," Human Rights Watch, New York, July 15, 2010; "Kazakhstan: Protect Detainees From Torture, Ill-Treatment," Human Rights Watch, New York, December 22, 2011.

16. *Ibid.,* Uildriks, pp. 8-10.

17. Multiple interviews with law enforcement officials, political leaders, and NGO activists in Kyrgyzstan and Kazakhstan, March-October 2012.

18. On how reforms are implemented in Saakashvili's government, see Thomas de Waal, "Georgia's Choices: Chart-

ing a Future in Uncertain Times," Washington, DC: Carnegie Endowment, 2011.

19. Interveiw with Levan Izoria, member of Alliance for Georgia and former rector of the Interior Ministry Academy (2004-06), Tbilisi, Georgia, February 2012.

20. Georgia's World Bank's Ease of Doing Business (ranking 16th out of 183 countries in 2011) and Transparency International (ranking 4.1 in 2011) ratings have improved over the past decade and are considerably higher compared to other former Soviet countries.

21. *Ibid.*; de Waal.

22. *Fighting Corruption in Public Services: Chronicling Georgia's Reforms*, Washington, DC: World Bank, January 2012, p. 13.

23. Matthew Delvin, "Seizing the Reform Moment: Rebuilding Georgia's Police, 2004-2006," *Innovations for Successful Societies*, 2010.

24. Matthew Light, "Police Reform, Civilian Control, and National Security in the Republic of Georgia (former USSR)," Paper presented at the annual meeting of The Law and Society Association, Renaissance Chicago Hotel, Chicago, IL, May 27, 2010.

25. *Ibid.*; Izoria.

26. For more on U.S. and international funding in Georgia, see Lincoln A. Mitchell, *Uncertain Democracy: U.S. Foreign Policy and Georgia's Rose Revolution*, Philadelphia, PA: University of Pennsylvania Press, 2009.

27. Interview with Tornike Turmanidze, then Deputy Secretary National Security Council, Tbilisi, Georgia, February 2012.

28. *Ibid.*; World Bank, p. 8.

29. "Georgia: The Risk of Winter," Crisis Group, Brussels, Belgium, November 26, 2008, p. 6.

30. "Blood Feud," *The Economist*, July 13, 2012.

31. Interview with Shota Utiashvili, former head of Georgian Interior Ministry's analytical department, Tbilisi, Georgia, February 2012.

32. *Ibid.*, interview with Turmanidze.

33. Interview with a patrol police officer who served since 2004, Tbilisi, Georgia, March 2012.

34. Interview, Tbilisi, Georgia, February 2012.

35. *Ibid.*, interview with Utiashvili. However, unlike commonly stereotyped, these employees were not fired in a single day; rather, it was done over a span of several months.

36. Interview with Gela Kvashilava, Deputy Director Department of Information and Analysis, Interior Ministry, Tbilisi, Georgia, March 2012.

37. *Ibid.*, interview with Utiashvili.

38. Interveiw with Khatia Dekanoidze, former head of Police Academy, Tbilisi, Georgia, March 2012.

39. *Ibid.*

40. *Ibid.*, World Bank, p. 18.

41. Interview with government official, Tbilisi, Georgia, March 2012.

42. *Ibid.*, interview with Dekanoidze.

43. *Ibid.*

44. *Ibid.*, interview with Utiashvili.

45. *Ibid.*

46. Utiashvili's estimate; according to the World Bank, during 2003-04, the share of Georgia's shadow economy to real GDP changed only slightly—from 65.9 percent to 62.1 percent. Friedrick Schneider *et al.*, "Shadow Economies All Over the World: New Estimates for 162 countries from 1992 to 2007," Policy Research Working Papers, 5359, July 2010.

47. Interview with NGO activists, Tbilisi, Georgia, June 2012.

48. Haley Sweetland Edwards, "Tajikin on Saakashvili," April 4, 2012, available from *atitude.blogs.nytimes.com*.

49. Jim Garamone, "U.S. to Provide $1 Billion for Georgia Reconstruction, Humanitarian Aid," American Forces Press Service, September 3, 2008.

50. Jim Nichol, "Georgia [Republic]: Recent Developments and U.S. Interest," Washington, DC: Congressional Research Service, July 13, 2012.

51. "Georgia: Attracting investments, contributing to economic growth," Washington, DC: Millenium Challenge Corporation, August 25, 2011.

52. Interview, representative of European External Action Service, Tbilisi, Georgia, June 2012.

53. *Ibid.*; Wold Bank, p. 14.

54. Larisa Burakova, *Pochemu u Gruzii poluchilos'? (Why Does It Work in Georgia?)*, Moscow, Russia: Al'pina biznes buks, 2011, p. 22.

55. *Ibid.*, p. 21.

56. "Police Reform is the Main Symbol of creating Georgian New Statehood," *InterPressNews*, December 28, 2009, available from *www.interpressnews.ge/en/politics/28129-police-reform-is-main-symbol-of-creating-georgian-new-statehood.html*.

57. "Saakashvili Praises Police, Interior Minister," *Civil Georgia*, May 6, 2012.

58. *Ibid.*

59. Interview with Eka Gigauri, head of Transparency International-Georgia, Tbilisi, Georgia, June 2012.

60. "Ex-Defense Minister Kezerashvili Accused of Corruption," January 31, 2013, available from *Civil.ge*; interview with Gigauri. Also see Lincoln A. Mitchell, "Uncertain Democracy: U.S. Foreign Policy and Georgia's Rose Revolution," University Park, PA: University of Pennsylvania State, 2008, chaps. 2 and 5.

61. Interview with Ekaterine Popkhadze, Executive Director, Georgian Young Lawyers' Association, Tbilisi, Georgia, June 2012.

62. *Ibid.*; interview with Gigauri.

63. Interview, Tbilisi, Georgia, June 2012.

64. Interview with corruption and development specialist, Tbilisi, Georgia, June 2012.

65. "Ivanishvili Warns Police against 'Fulfilling Illegal Orders'," *Civil Georgia*, May 5, 2012.

66. Nana Kurashvili, "Political Channel-Hopping in Georgia," July 8, 2012, available from *IWPR.net*.

67. "Public Defender Releases 2011 Human Rights Report," March 29, 2012, available from *Civil.ge*; "Public Defender Releases 2010 Human Rights Report," April 4, 2011, available from *Civil.ge*.

68. *Ibid.*, interview with Gigauri.

69. Interview with NGO activist, Tbilisi, Georgia, June 2012.

70. Interveiw with representative of Ombudsman's office, Tbilisi, Georgia, June 2012.

71. *Ibid.*, interview with Utiashvili.

72. "Crossing the Line: Georgia's Violent Dispersal of Protestors and Raid on Imedi Television," Human Rights Watch, December 20, 2007.

73. *Ibid.*, interview with NGO expert.

74. Interview, Tbilisi, Georgia, June 2012.

75. Ekaterine Popkhadze *et al.*, "Legal Analysis of Cases of Vriminal and Administrative Offences with Alleged Political Motive," GYLA, Tbilisi, Georgia, 2011.

76. *Ibid.*, World Bank, p. 10.

77. Interview with corruption and development specialist, Tbilisi, Georgia, June 2012.

78. "Georgia: Investigate Sexual Abuse in Prison," New York: Human Rights Watch, September 19, 2012.

79. Interview with police officer, Bishkek, Kyrgyzstan, May 2012.

80. Aziza Abdirasulova's presentation during Kyrgyz Interior Ministry Public Council meeting, Bishkek, Kyrgyzstan, September 2011.

81. Leila Saralaeva, "Akademiya MVD i 'Monte Karlo'," ("Interior Ministry Academy and 'Monte Karlo'"), July 6, 2012, available from *Chalkan.kg*.

82. Zairbek Baktybayev, "Kursanty MVD ustroili draku" (Interior Ministry Cadets Provoked a Fight), June 21, 2012, available from *Azattyk.org*.

83. *Ibid.*; Bloed.

84. Interview with NGO expert, Bishkek, Kyrgyzstan, June 2012.

85. Interview with representative of an international donor organization, Bishkek, Kyrgyzstan, June 2012.

86. David Lewis, *The Reassessment of the Role of OSCE Police Assistance Programming in Central Asia*, Central Eurasia Project, New York: OSI, April 2011.

87. Interview with MP Ravshan Jeenbekov, Bishkek, Kyrgyzstan, June 2012.

88. Voice of Freedom's interview with Kalicha Umuralieva, initiater of a working group on the police reform, available from *vof.kg/?p=4862*; interviews with several NGO activists, Bishkek, Kyrgyzstan, October 2011-June 2012.

89. *Ibid.*; Lewis, p. 17.

90. For more on corruption in Kyrgyzstan's state structures, see Johan Engvall, "Flirting with State Failure: Power and Politics in Kyrgyzstan since Independence," Washington, DC: Central Asia – Caucasus Institute & Silk Road Studies Program, July 2011.

91. *Ibid.*; Lewis, p. 10.

92. Jim Nichol, "Kyrgyzstan: Recent Developments and U.S. Interests," Washington, DC: Congressional Research Service, January 19, 2012.

93. White House, "Fact Sheet: U.S. Assistance to Kyrgyzstan," Washington, DC: The White House, September 24, 2010.

94. More details on early reform efforts is available from *www.mvd.kg/index.php?option=com_content&view=article&id=184&Itemid=68&lang=ru.*

95. *Ibid.*; Lewis, p. 31.

96. Interview with representative of Defense Ministry, Bishkek, Kyrgyzstan, October 2010.

97. Interview with Kyrgyz Interior Ministry official, Bishkek, Kyrgyzstan, May 2012.

98. More details are available from *www.mvd.kg/index.php? option=com_content&view=article&id=185&Itemid=69&lang=ru.*

99. Interview with Shamshibek Mamyrov, deputy head of the Chief Administration for Legal and Criminal Analysis at the Interior Ministry, Bishkek, Kyrgyzstan, September 2011.

100. During protests in central Bishkek, Kyrgyzstan, 95 were killed and hundreds injured by government troops.

101. Interview with NGO activist Kalicha Umuralieva, Bishkek, Kyrgyzstan, June 2012.

102. *Ibid.*

103. *Ibid.*; interview with Jeenbekov.

104. Erica Marat, "Kyrgyzstan: Bishkek Following Georgia's Lead of Police Reform," October 28, 2011, available from *Eurasia net.org.*

105. Interview with Kyrgyz MP, June 2012, Bishkek, Kyrgyzstan.

106. *Ibid.*, interview with Umuralieva.

107. "Timur Shaihutdinov: Reformiriovat' MVD bez obnovleniya kadrv nevozmozhno" ("Timur Shaihutdinov: It Is Impossible to Reform Interior Ministry without New Cadre"), *Voice of Freedom*, May 5, 2012, available from *vof.kg/?p=4725*; "Mirsuljan Namazaliev: 'Rezul'tat realizatsii Al'ternativnoi kontseptsii reformy MVD ne zastavit sebya zhdat'" (It Won't Be Long Before the Results of the Alternative Interior Ministry Reform Concept Will Be Seen), May 2, 2012, available from *K-news.kg.*

108. Interview with Kyrgyz Interior Ministry official, Bishkek, Kyrgyzstan, June 2012.

109. "Osnovnye polozheniya proekta Kontseptsii reformirovaniya organiv vnutrennih del Kyrgyzskoi Respubliki na period s 2012 g. por 2015 god" (The Main Positions of the Project of Kyrgyz

Republic's Interior Ministry Reform Concept for the Period from 2012 until 2015), unpublished version of the reform's concept.

110. *Ibid.*, interview.

111 . *Ibid.*; *Voice of Freedom.*

112. Multiple interviews with Kyrgyz Interior Ministry personnel, Bishkek, Kyrgyzstan, 2011-12.

113. *Ibid.*, *Voice of Freedom.*

114. Interview with rank-in-file policeman, Karakol, Kyrgyzstan, August 2008.

115. "Kalicha Umuralieva: 'Neobhodimo otkazat'sya ot praktiki prisvoeniya zvaniya generalov glavam MVD Kyrgyzstana'" ("Kalicha Umuralieva: 'It is necessary to get rid of the practice of assigning the rank of general to Interior Ministers of Kyrgyzstan'"), July 15, 2012, available from *www.24.kg.*

116. Multiple interviews with Kyrgyz Interior Ministry personnel, Bishkek, Kyrgyzstan, 2011-12.

117. Interveiw with GAI personnel, Bishkek, Kyrgyzstan, Septermber 2011.

118. Interview with a local policeman, Karakol, Kyrgyzstan, August 2009. The policeman drove "Nissan," but he hoped he'd be driving a "Lexus" if he was to be relocated to Osh.

119. More on this in *Ibid.*; Joshua Kucera, *U.S. Military Aid to Central Asia: Who Benefits?* New York: Open Society Foundation, September 2012.